MONEY MONEY MONEY
WATER WATER WATER

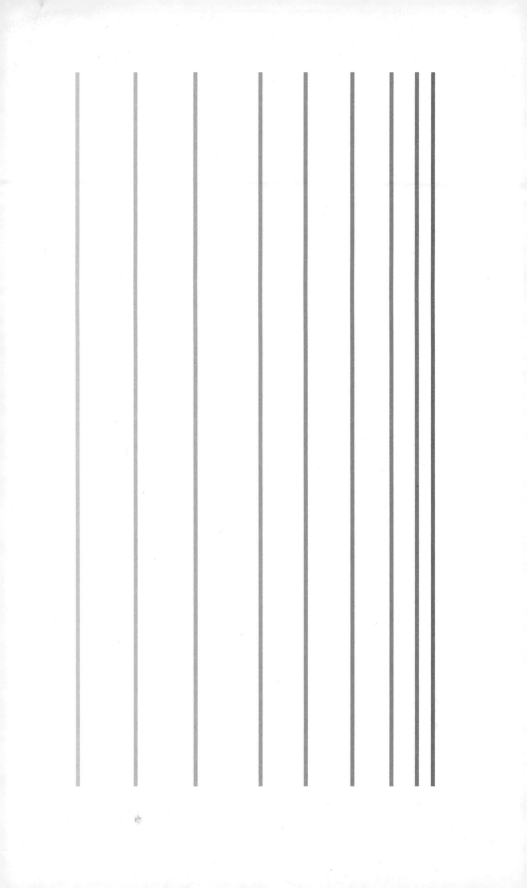

MONEY MONEY MONEY
WATER WATER WATER

a trilogy

Jane Mead

For Howard —
Another book
Lover — Jane
2015
Napa

ALICE JAMES BOOKS | FARMINGTON, MAINE

10 9 8 7 6 5 4 3 2 1

Alice James Books are published by Alice James Poetry Cooperative,
Inc., an affiliate of the University of Maine at Farmington.

ALICE JAMES BOOKS
114 PRESCOTT STREET
FARMINGTON, ME 04938

www.alicejamesbooks.org

Library of Congress Cataloging-in-Publication Data
Mead, Jane, 1958-
[Poems. Selections]
Money money money water water water / Jane Mead.
pages cm
ISBN 978-1-938584-04-6 (pbk.)
I. Title.
ps3563.e165m66 2014
811'.54--dc23

2013040148

Alice James Books gratefully acknowledges support from individual
donors, private foundations, the University of Maine at Farmington
and the National Endowment for the Arts.

ART WORKS.

COVER ART: "Aquifer Test," photo-geologic composite by Jonathon
Wells © 2006. earthexposure.net

CONTENTS

|

FALLEN LEAF LAKE

|

DOROTHY PRETENDING TO BE WATER
DOROTHY PRETENDING TO BE SKY

ACKNOWLEDGMENTS

MY WARM THANKS to the editors and staff of the following publications in which these poems first appeared (sometimes in earlier versions) for their generous support of this work and of contemporary poetry in general: *American Poetry Review, Columbia Poetry Review, Fifth Wednesday Journal, Great River Review, SEIZURE STATE (Gigantic), The Iowa Review, Passages North, Poetry, Poetry Daily, Poetry International, Scythe*, and *Tidepools*.

In addition, I am most grateful for the generous support of the Lannan Foundation and to the guardians of the Elizabeth Bishop House in Nova Scotia, for writing residencies during which this book began to take shape, and found its final form, respectively.

Ira, Jan, Jean, Kathleen, Betsey, Madeleine, Jerry, Ginny, Tess, Anne Marie, Lisa,—thank you my dear friends for your guidance with these poems, and for your good selves. Deep gratitude to Ramon Rodriguez, Silvia Rodriguez, Judi Ouellette, and Jim Clark, for making the writing of these poems possible, and to Carey Salerno, Meg Willing, Alyssa Neptune, Gale Mead, and Dede Cummings for your graciousness and wisdom while bringing this book into being; finally, my thanks to Julia Bouwsma, copyeditor extraordinaire,—unconventional punctuation and grammar are deliberate.

Also by Jane Mead

The Usable Field

House of Poured-Out Waters

The Lord and the General Din of the World

A Truck Marked Flammable (long poem,
published as a chapbook by State Street Press)

for toby and greg

Money money money
Water water water

—Theodore Roethke, "The Lost Son"

MONEY

Someone had the idea of getting more water
released beneath the Don Pedro Dam
into the once-green Tuolumne,—

so the minnows could have some wiggle room,
so the salmon could lunge far enough up
to spawn, so that there would be more salmon

in the more water below the dam.
But it wasn't possible—by then the water
didn't belong to the salmon anymore, by then

the water didn't even belong to the river.
The water didn't belong to the water.

THAT THE CHURCH OF ENGLAND
SHOULD BE FREE

WE APPROACH MAGNA CARTA

We approach Magna Carta from six degrees
of separation, but we approach her.
Serfs one minute, slaves the next—

and where's the shore from there?
In the interim, accounts are kept—
memories washed up to live with.

What greater claim?
What monumental difficulty—
turning law into democracy—

and then all this embedded shame.
Even the chapter on Culture Today—
that part written by some geezer

with secret ties to the monarchs.
Custom Today: sandy craters
in color, fallen walls.

All those children with no arms.
All those myths exploding.
Still, there is all manner of knowing

in the manor house—like:
Loam to be found in the quarters
where the slaves live!

+

Books of grasses books of scat
Books of rodents books of tracks
Books of sadness books of flight

How much how much where going

HUMAN OF THE FIRST FORGIVEN,

seven of the flowers,——
balancing our wages with
our ways, our unremarkable

days, (six through mist).
Thirty caves dug into
the hillside, unforgiving

repertoire of chipping. Then
ceiling-roots as new beginnings:
Then just who-so-ever,

and so-on and so-forth
all over again. Whomsoever
as the Earth's rattled

inheritance. Seedpods!
Thirty books in which
the variables were hidden:

the hybrid pelt, the edible
heirloom, etc. encircling
the lair of governance, damp

and clay-like ceiling cracking.
Thirty caves where the failures go.
Chirping under stones. Echo.

+

Smell of lavender and bay
Smell of hemispheres of thinning
Universe of years within me

Message hidden hidden nowhere

LASSITUDE AND INDEPENDENCE

The electrical plant (acres of desert)—
(we came to) and it wasn't long and we came
to the white crater of the borax plant.

The light a (post-desire) landscape (post-verdant)—
the clean bone (the sun) the day-winds (the night):
the mind gives over its small grave of secrets:

this is the way to know what you know:
determine the future history of clouds—
study (valleys) rock escarpments and canyons—.

The green world enters, introduces its yellows—
(no false reckoning, no plan, no artifice)—
the light as landscape (the specter as shore):

this is the way to know what you know:
the mind gives over its small grave of secrets—.

+

Complexity of thistle and desire
Maybe a million things maybe nothing
My heart somewhere in the musty grasses

Wishes nothing who wishes stone

SOLIDS AND NON-SOLIDS

The air is solids and non-solids.
The person is solids and non-solids:
Solids and non-solids all the way down.

Halo of leaves. Aura of notes.
No kidding. All the way down.
Forgotten and not forgotten.

Candle. Matches. Needle. Down.
The old-fashioned stream remains.
The mind remains, thinking *lost*

lost, loster—all the way down.

+
Water-borne poison
Poison borne by air
Data on dead animals

Angry children on the move

COVE

*

Lithonate is some sort of lithium
and crawling is some sort of life.
I don't know how they do it elsewhere

but here we all try to be awfully good
—and still sometimes they lock us up.
Life made proper isn't what you think.

Where the woods meet the cove
there should be a sentence written in stone—
far enough back so the water can't get it,

push it around with its mindless rippling.
Meanwhile, leaves turn on their axes of air—
i.e.: it is fall: the straw-colored fields

are useless now, and the woods, too—useless,
with their loud display: if they want
anything it's to be left alone—left out

of the poem, allowed to die in peace.

+

The creation of want
The creation of debt
The creation of the toxic ponds

If they wave wave back

**

I'm no lover of human skin in any shade.
I prefer the animals who live
without their souls—how there's nothing

that floats away on a sea of sky
like a *what-did-you-say-we-were* by and by.
Hell, I don't even know what I am

right now,—a forgettable fact?
I don't know *a thing*, but I like
to hope I'll get this figuring figured—

that God will lean out of some cloud
bellowing my name, waving my ribbon.
Oh hell. Have mercy on us—

someone. Anyone. Anyone who is watching.
Save up. Save us. (*Big job.*)

+

Ditch company to sell shares
Shares of water to Audubon
For bird habitat on terms

Elsewhere offered to lettuce farmers

***

There ought to be a path with a promise—
it's a kiss with a sense of closure,
it's a graceful way to die.

If you've got something that stands
for prayer, roll it on down the road
in my direction—I'll be standing

at the rim of the patient and organized
forest, to the left of a quaking aspen.
I'll be scanning the horizon for a smudge

of myself. Roll it on down—
I like to watch things wobble.

+

A gray and helpless stringency
Bootstraps gone missing
Patterns of light on the dog

A home for the omen

****

I was raised on the enlightened consumerism
of upper bohemia, fell from grace into
lower bohemia—which is defined by

an inability to take adult responsibility:
don't sell *me* anything on credit.
In fact, don't sell me anything at all.

Thank you. Now listen here—
I took the workshop on basic functioning,
studied the universal precautions

and the diagram of the evacuation plan,
I sent away for the free booklet
on why I was born. You can trust me

with your children now—the eggs
are hidden in the bushes to signify
rebirth, bread in the oven, beans

on the stove, knife in the drawer.
To signify rebirth.

+

Rancher paid to forgo
Forgo third cutting of hay
To leave water in the streams

For late-summer fish flows

*****

I came out of the dark hills
and the dark hills own me. I have
no patience for the sticky-minded

stratums. The concern of the comfortable
for the comfortable makes me sick. Meanwhile,
the red leaves spin on their axes of air,

different leaves now, different axes,
same big death. And wouldn't we love
to shrug now and just say sorry?

Apparently not say sorry.
Let's not talk about it.
I wish I lived in an opium cloud.

+

Make way for seeing
Make way for blindness
Make way for the vision

Of sea caught in cove

******

Listen—it's all the same:
the world in the needle,
the iron in the iron-colored sky.

There's a cove in every leaf.
Don't ask *me* how it got there
but it's like our love for thin air,

the distraction of the kiss, our hope
for something beyond what we can
plainly see—the poisoned planet poisoning.

Kmart may just well be as successful
an organization as we're up to.
But if I could tell you how to live

chances are I'd get drunk instead
and turn into some kind of stand-up
comic, say *look!*—*the rust is unfurling*

as far as the human eye can see!

+

The greater part of the world
World upon us
Upon us the greater part

of terror

THE NARROWS

And if you cannot start
with one true thing? And if
you cannot start? If, after

the *search and rescue* paradigm
and the paradigm of *either/or*,
you are not yet perplexed

by the transport of being,—
you are at the place I call
the narrows; it is time

for a picnic in the car,
in the rain, on the cliffs
overlooking the ocean. It is

time to hear the winded
rain against the windows
and know that not far away

the ocean is in angry mourning
and that you, for all
your wind and rain, cannot

even begin to hear it.

+

Fading elasticity of spirit
In the bone-house made
I would make from this poison

House of light and birds

EXPERIENCE AS VISITATION

That which comes unwilled comes shining—
    Pulls up the sun from out dark waters,
Moves through mist, a mind in motion—
    (There is a harbor there, within you).

(Comes unwilled, comes shining)—
    Wolves lift their heads to ghost-sound,
The bird inside the box, calling—
    (Rose, birdcall, wind—come shining).

Comes of nothing, comes unbidden—
    The lunar and the mutual mission,
The mutual order and the lack—
    (Every ruptured and unclaimed fact).

That which comes unbidden comes directly—
    (Comes unleashed, uncharted and—comes shining).

+

Books of fact books of shadow
Books of poems books of prose
If you want to revisit the house of bones

Don't ask me to come with you

MAGNA CARTA

That the church of England should be free—
And have her whole rights and liberties, inviolable—
The city of London shall have her liberties and free customs—
All Archbishops, Bishops, Abbots, Priors, Templars—
Shall have their liberties and free customs—

All Hospitallers, Earls, Barons and all Persons—
As well Spiritual as well Temporal—
Shall have their free liberties and free customs—
And the cities and burroughs and towns—
And the Barons of the Five Ports and all other ports—

One measure of Wine shall be through our realm—
And one measure of Ale, and one measure of Corn—
And one breadth of dyed Cloth, that is to say—
Two Yards and it will be of Weights as it is of Measures—

+
If they wave wave back
If they falter hide
If they linger stay hidden

Stay hidden

MAYBE LATER

Who enrages maybe later—
Who watches over enrages—
Delicate Laws Of The Aftermath—

Delicate clatter: however—
However there are still children—
However the last gasp gasping *children*—

An unforgivable innocence for later—
They are a brand of aftermath—
Later we will all be equal—

Cedar fell and neutral under rain—
Nation of clatter and tremble—
Of he-who-watches-over remember—

+

Numbered keys on numbered nails
Numbered days in numbered years
Innumerable flies on the fawn the dog killed

Two dark mules in memory

MAGNIFICENT DEFENDER
OF THE AFTERMATH

knows fate's a sure device, says
it's the world of the word—therein:
not wager, not sin, fate. The dead

explore the coastlines, grays
and charcoals excluded, roots—excluded,
and the drift and moor of elsewhere

temporarily, it seems, forbidden. They
come and go, walking their circles
around us, walking out a little

into the thick of it, the thicket of
a little ice storm, a little hay-stack,—
a little nay-saying thicket. Ticket out.

+
I can't hear the whisper
I can barely feel the breath
Elsewhere gnats drinking

Drinking from the eyes of children

TINTORETTO NATIVITY

(canvas painted over, 1550s)

The angel has been chopped in half
and his legs covered over. The legs
of Christ on the cross have been
painted over. The rocks on which
the main figures sit were clouds.

——MUSEUM PLAQUE

+

Some rise up from ash as greenery
Some as a darker measure of being
Some go as water some as day

Some refuse even to say their names

TAMOXIFEN

My mother gives me her earrings—
and a ring. We sort through
shells and sand, we kneel

in salt water, we nap.
We are two women
in the shade a cliff makes.

The sun paints the water.
The wind paints the sand.
In every direction, gulls cry.

It was never a question
of what they were for—
the sand and the sea, the pearl

on the pink shell of an ear—
but they sent her back
from the eclipse and she

didn't come back. Just
as blue is an illusion
for sky, just as the wind

takes the fog out, just
how we say it: *doorless,*
doorless,—then *stay.*

+
Lost the sky within the blade
The blade within the loam
The thought within the dome of days

Lost the dome of days

VACUUM DRAMA

Or stay alive in drama of houses
and dogs,—old paintings
of cows, small fast cars,

exploding, but not before a swirl
down the twisted coastline.
And if the sea isn't the thing?

No to the steaming horizon then.
No to fear eating the life.
Flashy Gnostic suck-hole returning:

  —*Hello* darling-black sunshine.
  —*Hello* moon-black sunshine.
  —Black flame-of-the-sun, *hello:*

the children of memory are dreams.
I'd say the sea *is* the thing.
Or the muddy grasses, the broken egg.

Or singing on the landing!
The herons have no knowledge of this—
save the narrows of the river,

the straits between the bay and ocean.
Which is, of course, the thing:
the whisper and the breathing.

All that beauty. All that dreaming.

+

Was too a story passing through
The bird outside my sister rapture
Later a house where the bees can stay

Lizard my rapture watching

DUST AND RUMBLE

No one could predict such dust and rumble.
Neither applying oneself well nor badly.
The line between us, three feet agape:

Loma Prieta or doubt—no telling.
The only break, the break as forgotten.—
I saw it in my own mind with you

on the other side as a mistake.
Who thought we could create
such dust and rumble, who thought

all we needed was a clean slate,
level ground, and a bag of marbles.
Forgotten, the only break in the break.

+

Books of names books of flowers
Books of trees books of hours
Books of dead books of living

How much less where going

FALLEN LEAF LAKE

DYING OF STUPIDITY

Dying of stupidity we want must muster something—
Nothing stepping forward, nothing forgetting:
The subsequent prying a disaster, a bloodletting.

Anaesthetizing clatter where once we carried upward—
Neither to enlarge our souls nor put the world out—
Who watches over, let us go somewhere now together.

I think there is one oak for every millionth child,
One glass of water (human or god) for every millionth child.
Neither to enrage, defend or compensate—neither nor *nor*.

What cross now bearing, what shadow throwing.
How much less where going, the object of love?
Good and Evil in quotes? How hard can it be.

+
Lamb saying flies on my eyes
Saying shit in my fur
Dark sounds caught in my throat

Her heart of fire gone now

FALLEN LEAF LAKE

—For my grandfather

And we are looking for his spirit-home.
In the dark we walk this way and that.
In the high dark mountains of fire season

we walk this way and that.

The tall pines with their rough bark
smell of brown sugar and vanilla.
The dry needles slip under our feet.

In the hot dark of fire season.
Next to the lake in the shape of a leaf.
We are looking for his spirit-home.

We are looking for his—grave, yes.

+

Cluttered lair of the forgotten
Not I the one but I the many
How much more-so where going

The object of love

THE GEESE

slicing this frozen sky know
where they are going—
and want to get there.

Their call, both strange
and familiar, calls
to the strange and familiar

heart, and the landscape
becomes the landscape
of being, which becomes

the bright silos and snowy
fields over which the nuanced
and muscular geese are calling.

+

The greater part of the season of rain
Upon us the greater part of loss
Me in my forgetfulness

You betraying matter

PROSODY

Fatso, lard-ass, pig-face, tub

is what they mostly called him
that year he failed P.E.
and religion,—the year
his mother's house burnt down

which was also the year of the flood.

Till then he'd thought of life
as a meaningful motion toward song—.

These days, if you ask him,
he'll just grin, shrug—

say *music is as music does*.

+

This is the pod of the sweetgum
That is the flood plane
This is the housefly from hell

That is an old Chevrolet

THE MULE DEER ON THE HILLSIDE
THE RIVER DREAM
THE HISTORY

*

Where is my lover now
if not in history?

The boats are on the river
still, as I dreamed them—

and the mule deer
dip their muzzles

into the bucket and lift
them up, dripping

in the heat-smeared summer
while elsewhere

the dry grasses smoke
and crackle.

+

Then he pulled his own red cap
Over the boy's head and together
They stopped weeping

Weeping and walked on

**
John says the dead
and the living share
the same world, only

the living do not know it.
The deer we named Argonaut
lifts his mule-face

into his deer-history,
and his deer-thoughts shine:
chewing, unblinking

he considers me gravely.

\+

When the birds fall out of the sky
And the fish wash up on the shore
Come and get me we'll ask for more

The use of the human body as spirit

***

The doe we named
for her fence-scars,
the doe we named

for her broken ear,
the tiny doe we named
for the white inside

her legs, along
her belly and her
twin, still spotted

fawns, lie under the oaks—
heads high, composed.
This water. *This* air.

+

While we were sleeping
The boy in the red cap exchanged
The dead bird for a living bird

Then bicycled on down the road

****

With what besides the soul
could you believe the body

has a voice? We put
the body of that rattler

on the stone pillar
by the drive, an offering

for the raptors if they'd
have her. When I went back

for the head, it clamped
my rusty shovel blade.

+
The heavens open the birds
Birds drop down from the sky
The oceans and bays deliver

Their stars and fish to the shore

*****

And there's the rattler-buzz
the mole imitates
in her panic, hands

blindly paddling the air
while Toby snaps her spine
four times, drop of blood

tipping her long nose
the way milk beaded
on the nose of the mouse

we found, still blind—
in the sun-scorched vineyard,
rowing in his darkness

for all he was worth
and not a nest in sight.
Where is my lover's body now

if not in history, in sky,
in the scent of vinegar grass
and the dry-smelling chaparral.

+
Do you remember our little boat
The father said to his boy
On the bed—the boy's mind

Thus occupied he died

THE GIFT

Whether you think of life
as gates and bridges, or traps
in the form of doors

left open; whether you
are waiting for the snap
of neck, or for the arc

of light—by which to measure
your horizon (caper of particles
and motion); whether you know

or not that the great
enthrallment may or may not
be coming: death says

listen for the echo. Begin
with thunderstorms and move
slowly toward the calm wherein

white trumpets of amaryllis
sag in the sticky dusk—
listen for the soundtrack

of the echo in the weather.

+
Unruffled un-trusted unheard
Unheard from sea-marsh unfailing beach
Undeveloped seedpods unhoused

I come unhoused

SPIRIT'S

got a stone around its noose,—
goodbye to *maybe*, goodbye
to *artifact* and *challenge*.

Artifice and *act* reviving.
Noose coming up empty. Net
coming up empty. Spirit's

not a stone, but a noose
releasing. Daemon's
a death-wish rethinking. Me?

I am neither here nor elsewhere,—
abandoned unto utter abandon.

+

Their laughter was their only own land
Once you start carrying your wounded
Wounded it's a different story

A mute pretending after another elsewhere

INCOMPLETE SCENARIO
INVOLVING FIRE AND WATER

Authority: off
somewhere in the dark
wings, conducting terror.

The smart daughter,
too—off in the wings
with her startling

ineptitude and her shame.
The strong daughter alone
is doing well though

she has neglected
her patrol—how else explain
the house, in flames.

And how explain
what keeps you
from going the way

of the dining-room table,
that gorgeous
inferno, but to mention

the white husky.
Who that white dog?
And *where* the shimmering

over the bay of clear sailing?

+

In a remote and steamy ocean
I lost my mother
She is not haze not mist

She is that pure

THE BIRD THAT KEEPS
THE SLOW BOY SPINNING

The bird that keeps
the slow boy spinning—
is extinct: though the boy

with the chapped face
crosses our streets, though
it is *our* spattered fenders

that hit him, he is
listening to the bird from
the other landscape, the bird

that never arrives—
the way we keep circling
long after we die.

+

Looking for a gravesite
Hoping for a major notion
Watercress ditch-side

Where the old spring fades

THE ELEPHANTS IN THE OCHRE CLAY

The ochre elephants
did not fail me,—I failed
to meet them half way.

Therefore I cannot envision
them entire, just trunks
in ochre sway: an inhuman

account of beauty, a pattern
for the oceans to pick up on
and with which the wind might play.

+

Wisdom you've forgotten
Garden of wisdom we've forgotten
The bird in yesterday

Almost the bird in tomorrow

WALKING, BLUES

Rain so dark I
can't get through—
train going by

in a hurry. The voice
said *walk or die*, I
walked,—the train

and the voice all
blurry. I walked with
my bones and my heart

of chalk, not even
a splintered notion:
days of thought, nights

of worry,—lonesome
train in a hurry.

+
Going to town for vodka at noon
Turning the ghost away
The heart a lump of meat

Meat in its nest of fluid

WE GO FROM LIGHT INTO DARKNESS
WITH BARELY A WORD TO SAY

Despair, that wash
of nightmare—
returning: if it

does not kill
you, you will
come to the day

when a crow makes
a vision of the
lemon tree—kind

of moment you'd
give a life for—
(Just see to it

that it does
not kill you.)

+

Now as animal bodies
As the glistening fur
Fur in the rain smells

Let us smell

STALKING THE PLEASURES

The pleasures are the *can-be*
and the *want*, the abundance
of water before the well

went dry. The pleasures
are primitive stalks of *might-be*
and *aftermath*, shaded

and bamboo-like grasses
on the arduous walk
to the waterfall: first

brush so thick we crawl,
then down into the dense
and muggy grasses, muddy

elbows and no idea where
the path is—stalking
the pleasures: *heart-beat*

can-be, stone's-throw, want.

+
There was only one egg
One hard-boiled egg
And Akhmatova

Gave it to Mandelstam

DOROTHY PRETENDING
TO BE WATER

DOROTHY PRETENDING
TO BE SKY

THE LENGTH OF LIFE

*

There is the risk of touching and shrieking.
(There is mist on the pond,—so I watch it.)

I know I should be elsewhere, talking.
(Everyone else is elsewhere, talking.)

Mostly, they talk about touching and shrieking.
Sometimes it's oysters and snowmobiles.

+

The European grapevine moth task force
Recommends the deployment
Of mating disruption pheromone products

Products prior to the first flight

**

A thought rocked me gently to sleep once.
(Not a truth, but a universe.)

Then there was shrieking, and I lost it for always.
Years later, I asked my sleep to guide me.

The way was found to be quicksand
and the surrounding light—was blinding.

+
First generation flights begin
Near bud-break adults live
One to three weeks

Fly at dusk mate in flight

***

Mist on the pond where a scene is missing.
This is the forward-marching of history?

(The air that holds the mist is real.)
(Science says the mist is real.)

(The myth of history outlives science.)
Probably, I should be elsewhere—talking.

+

Infested clusters shrivel
Fully excavated berries dry
Fungal invaders are present

Last males trickling in

****

The girl in the tunic passes raw tuna——.
The guests all agree: the ocean is true.

The men are experts on parts of real oysters.
The women are experts in drawing the parts.

(Mother drew them to scale with an ivory ruler.)
Counties of color——in black and white.

+

7 May conventional insecticides
Continue to hold up well Altacor
Dipel Lannate Intrepid Brigade

Delegate Renounce Entrust Success

*****

Later, the way was found to be quicksand.
(Read history, read water, read pond—read myth.)

I told this first as The History Of Dark Waters.
(There was plenty of touching and plenty of shrieking.)

I offer it to you as comedy.
(I lost the one friend who knew it was funny.)

+

Timing and treatment of third flight
Of European grapevine moth is pending
The red dirt avenues the gibbous moon

I waver burdensome re spraying

******

There is always the risk of shrieking and lightning.
The way may be found to be quicksand or sight.

My mother gave me an ivory ruler.
My father gave me a labyrinth to live by.

The way may be found to be myth, to be history,—.
(Mist on the pond, where the scene is missing.)

+

Larva samples at ag office
Weight tags at department of weights
As in department of weights and measures

As in Bureau of Water Reclamation

LIKE A BLIND MAN
I CROUCH DOWN

My mother pots or doesn't pot the soil.
In the cold rain, I crouch down.
My ears are clean, but there's a boil
on my elbow and soil
under my nails, crusty and blood-brown.

December rains gather, froth and boil—
the river runs brown with topsoil.
On the road the earthworms stretch and drown.
(My ears are clean but there's a boil
where my heart should be and soil
in the flashing waterfalls near town.
My lover tilled or didn't till that soil.)

Loyal, disloyal, loyal, disloyal,
loyal. I flip my penny to the ground.
My forehead's mud-streaked. There's a boil
where the icy waters rise and roil.

In the field, the field mice drown.
My brother loves or doesn't love the soil.
In the field the narrow ditches boil.

+

The story of a place is a crooked story
The story of a family is worse
In the valley a thousand lights

And every light a failure

FROM THE FAMOUS CASTLE
OF NONEXISTENCE

*

I looked up one day
and saw my father creating
his soul by loving

the souls of trees.
It became easy then
to look for yellow

in the woods—easy
to call that looking
faithful to all things.

+

So what was the best way
What the way without I
Green pods of the walnut tree

Spiked and overhead

**

On the second day
the yellow dogs
come out of the woods

to play with me and Alice—
they surprise us. After that
there is a smallness in us

within which we are waiting.

+

Down Toby's trail to the burr-filled meadow
Up Alice's burr-filled trail to the ridge
Toby and Alice as dogs when we leave

On our return—Toby and Alice as bushes

MOWING AND AFTERMATH

Shock of rocks on the metal blades now:
(We left the corral gate open.
We let the weeds grow high.)

The orange falls into the house finch nest.
Small dog skips up the vineyard:
Reptiles and rodents to demolish, demolished!!

The lesser hope is the greater burden.
I could not my own fool life abandon.
No sun, no moon, no mowing?

No mustard disked under for mustard gas?
Turtles all the way down writes the monk.
And what kind of support system is *that.*

+

The world full of tractors
Is the mystery world
The other world

Is the seasons

STILL LIFE AND
STILL LIVING

*

Cabernet to the right.
Zinfandel to the left.
Slope and tilt of

the red road through
the north vineyard—
quirky passage I've been

for fifty years, where now
the girl-dog Alice
and the vineyard-master

Ramon are circling our best
tractor as if it were
a philosophical problem.

+

Three a ton or five an acre
He pulls leaves he drops fruit
Five a ton or eight an acre

We pull leaves we drop fruit

**

The turtle at the willows
doesn't know: water
table dropping, water

hole shrinking every
year where the wild
rhododendron bloom.

In that tiny whorl of
her thought—there's
barely enough mist

to get lost in—
so she keeps bumping along
as if there were no

problem: for she is one
of the sturdier gifts
on this mission.

+

He sells his handshake he breaks his word
He sputters over his sputtering jet
He thinks I'm a girl and can't do math

And he can kiss my lily-white ass

TOBY THE STRAY

The crown of his head smelled of redwood boughs
where he wiped his eyes in the morning.
The bottom of his feet smelled like brown sugar.

Through summer grasses, through winter fog
we set our compass on his white tail, waving.
The crown of his head smelled of redwood boughs.

He tipped his nose into the breeze, took his readings,
thanked me for dinner, snoozed on his back. Happiness
was his calling, and his feet smelled like brown sugar.

Close in the night, the coyotes fell silent
when he loosed his deep bark. There was a white heart
on the crown of his head. (It smelled of redwood boughs.)

He survived: scorpions, rattler bite, hound paralysis
and tick fever (twice). He showed me where my heart is,
and the bottom of his feet smelled like brown sugar.

He squeaked when he yawned, he sighed when he slept—
our bear, our lion, our soft-eyed prince.
The crown of his head smelled of redwood boughs
and the bottom of his feet like brown sugar.

+

Dream of patterns of light on the dog
Several omissions missing
And somewhere still a willow

By a well that marked a grave

BIG OR SMALL WITH LANGUAGE—

the seasons heave along is how
the seasons are heaving. Sun
on the reddening grape leaves

is sun on the red-leaf virus.
Take it. Knot in the oak
where the wasps stay, upturned

bucket by the old barn, a toad-castle
for the doughy blinker with his
one fast pulsing chin. I give you

the scorpion's scuttling shadow
in moonlight—the rattler
stretched long on the warm drive

at dusk: people love images and I
want some of that love for myself.
In the clouds a nest is forming.

The barn is faded red, barn-red
and mossy. The rattler, Mojave
rattler-gray and dusty. The heart

unravels—big or small with language
doesn't the heart unravel.

+

The dream-door darkens
The world repeals itself
The dark participants repeal

The air is lavish with moisture

THE DOWN AND DIRTY KEEP-AWAY GAME
FOR THE EATEN OR JUST MISSING

I am listening for the souls of foxes
  —Down and dirty
Foxes I knew, then gone one day
  —Eaten or just missing
They leapt and played one dawn
  —whom we named Jane and Greg
They pounced on mice, nibbled seed
  —shake rattle and roll
The cat along that limb's a lion
  —eaten or just missing
Palace of light and branches
  —leaping foxes summer dawn
In the greenhouse bedroom where love began
  —began.

+
Here the doe-faced dog
Here the fawn the Dane killed
Here my father's ashes

In the bone-dry field

A SONG FOR ALICE
IN THE RAINY SEASON

You will not go to a watery grave,
You will not go to your grave with ticks—
But you will go to your grave today.

Little dog who would never behave,
Who heard us call and watched, transfixed—
You will not go to a watery grave.

To the sheep you were a blurred crime-wave,
(Puzzled by dogs who chased after sticks)—
And spirited off to your grave today.

You led the other dogs astray,
Woke the neighbors, killed their chicks—
But you will not go to a watery grave.

Before we make your nest of hay
We line the flooded pit with bricks—
For you will go to your grave today.

We line the hay with twigs of bay.
I brush your tail. I check for ticks.
You will not go to a watery grave—
But you *will* go to your grave today.

+

Tadpoles on the flats
Vernal pools shrinking
Rocks we balanced on returning

We were a story passing through

BEEN A GRAPEVINE IN MY STEAD

In the end you *are*
and then after some time
you *are not*, more or less—

as the saying goes. What
did you want? You
who were barely honored

with birth in the first
place, who nearly missed
being in this world, *you*

when there could have been
a grapevine in your stead?

+

Tug and swoop of the grape-hook
Blade a thumbnail moon
Yellow-jackets on the sticky fruit

With or without worship——truth

DOROTHY AND JANE IN TESUQUE

Dorothy pretending to be water.
Dorothy pretending to be
sky. In the wide arroyo

under cottonwoods. With electrical
lines and without. With Forgiveness
and without. We were girls—

we were beautiful children.
For good measure, we stole apples.
We cut strands of barbed wire

for our ponies' passage. The prow,
when there was a prow, cut through
green waters of the Indian

reservoirs where heron stopped
in spring. Sometimes the dream-mask
shifted: bone-bruise and blood-clot,

seepage. The cliffs were red clay—
folds of shadow and light, home
to small rodents. Mystery

with neither name nor notice,
brackish river, world of salt
cedar, a rot-out tree, bee-nested.

Now, pour the honey down my throat—
thistle-ditch of darkness, dream-door
to the sun: ours, the pit and sink

to nowhere. And nowhere my blind body.

+

Magnificent defender of skies
Magnificent defender of oceans
How much can you subtract now

How much and still get by

Notes

|

MAGNA CARTA: the poem is composed entirely of phrases from Magna Carta.

TAMOXIFEN: Tamoxifen is a drug used to treat cancer. Wile taking it, my mother spoke of feeling emotionally "wooden."

Was too a story passing through: "The bird outside my sister rapture" is a variation on a line by Amanda Lichtenberg.

DUST AND RUMBLE: The Loma Prieta earthquake of 1989 was caused by slippage along the San Andreas Fault and was responsible for 69 deaths and much damage in the San Francisco Bay area.

THE MULE DEER, **: "John" refers to John Berger in *Hold Everything Dear: Dispatches on Survival and Resistence.*

"When the birds fall out of the sky / And the fish wash up on the shore" is a reference to the literal, mystifying instances of just such occurrences in recent years.

MOWING AND AFTERMATH: When mowed and disked under, mustard plant, the traditional cover crop in vineyards, produces mustard gas, which kills nematodes and other parasitic organisms.

Recent Titles from Alice James Books

|

Orphan, Jan Heller Levi
Hum, Jamaal May
Viral, Suzanne Parker
We Come Elemental, Tamiko Beyer
Obscenely Yours, Angelo Nikolopoulos
Mezzanines, Matthew Olzmann
Lit from Inside: 40 Years of Poetry from Alice James Books,
Edited by Anne Marie Macari and Carey Salerno
Black Crow Dress, Roxane Beth Johnson
Dark Elderberry Branch: Poems of Marina Tsvetaeva,
A Reading by Ilya Kaminsky and Jean Valentine
Tantivy, Donald Revell
Murder Ballad, Jane Springer
Sudden Dog, Matthew Pennock
Western Practice, Stephen Motika
me and Nina, Monica A. Hand
Hagar Before the Occupation | Hagar After the Occupation, Amal al-Jubouri
Pier, Janine Oshiro
Heart First into the Forest, Stacy Gnall
This Strange Land, Shara McCallum
lie down too, Lesle Lewis
Panic, Laura McCullough
Milk Dress, Nicole Cooley
Parable of Hide and Seek, Chad Sweeney
Shahid Reads His Own Palm, Reginald Dwayne Betts
How to Catch a Falling Knife, Daniel Johnson
Phantom Noise, Brian Turner
Father Dirt, Mihaela Moscaliuc
Pageant, Joanna Fuhrman
The Bitter Withy, Donald Revell

Alice James Books has been publishing poetry since 1973 and remains one of the few presses in the country that is run collectively. The cooperative selects manuscripts for publication primarily through regional and national annual competitions. Authors who win a Kinereth Gensler Award become active members of the cooperative board and participate in the editorial decisions of the press. The press, which historically has placed an emphasis on publishing women poets, was named for Alice James, sister of William and Henry, whose fine journal and gift for writing went unrecognized during her lifetime.

Designed by Dede Cummings

Printed by Thompson-Shore
on 30% postconsumer recycled paper
processed chlorine-free